Ellen MacArthur

Mike Wilson

Published in association with The Basic Skills Agency

A MEMBER OF THE HODDER HEADLINE GROUP

Acknowledgements
Photo credits
p.iv © Stephen Munday/Allsport/Getty Images; p.7 © John Downing/Rex Features;
p.12 © Stephen Hird/Reuters/Corbis; p.23 © John Downing/Rex Features;
p.27 © Adrian Sherratt/Rex Features

Every effort has been made to trace all copyright holders, but if any have been
inadvertently overlooked the Publishers will be pleased to make the necessary
arrangements at the first opportunity.

Orders: please contact Bookpoint Ltd, 130 Milton Park, Abingdon, Oxon OX14 4SB.
Telephone: (44) 01235 827720. Fax: (44) 01235 400454. Lines are open 9.00–6.00, Monday
to Saturday, with a 24-hour message answering service. Visit our website at
www.hoddereducation.co.uk

© Mike Wilson 2006
First published in 2006 by
Hodder Murray, an imprint of Hodder Education,
a member of the Hodder Headline Group
338 Euston Road
London NW1 3BH

Impression number   10 9 8 7 6 5 4 3 2 1
Year   2010 2009 2008 2007 2006

Cover photo © MARCEL MOCHET/AFP/Getty Images
Map supplied by Barking Dog Art
Typeset in 14pt Palatino by SX Composing DTP, Rayleigh, Essex
Printed in Great Britain by CPI, Bath

A catalogue record for this title is available from the British Library

ISBN-10: 0 340 91410 6
ISBN-13: 978 0340 914 106

Contents

Ellen (third from right, standing) with the Royal Yachting Association Youth Squad Masterclass.

Introduction

When Ellen MacArthur was eight years old,
her auntie took her sailing.
It was Ellen's first time on the sea,
and she fell in love with it.

She loved the sound of the wind
and the water.
She loved the smell of the boat,
the smell of the sea.

They sailed all day.
They sailed so far from land,
all they could see was water and sky.

Ellen had never felt so free.

From that day,
sailing was all she cared about.
Sailing was all she thought about.

1

Ellen was born on 8 July 1976
in a little village near Derby.
Derby is in the Midlands –
as far as you can get from the sea.

Yet Ellen knew
she'd found her true home.

She began saving her pocket money
to get a boat of her own.
Every weekend, every holiday,
Ellen went sailing.

A few years later,
Ellen MacArthur sailed round the world
and into the record books.

She was just 24 years old,
and only five feet two inches (1 metre 58cm).

This is the story of a little girl
from a village near Derby,
the boats she sailed,
and how she won her place in history.

1 *The Kestrel*

The Kestrel
was Ellen's first real sailing boat.

Before that,
she had a little dinghy,
just eight feet (2.5m) long.

It was parked in the garden
most of the time.
Ellen would sit on the dinghy,
there in the garden.
She tied the ropes
and changed the sails.

Her bedroom wasn't big enough
for all the ropes and sails.
Ellen took the bed out,
and slept on the floor.

She dreamed of the sea.

When she got *The Kestrel*,
Ellen learned to sail.

At weekends and in holidays,
she went on courses.
She got qualifications.
She learned how to handle a boat.
She learned how to read a map at sea.
She learned how to read the sea
and the sky.

Ellen had to learn
how to repair boats as well.

The Kestrel was old.
Ellen had to repair bits of the deck,
the keel, the pump and the cabin.

Years later,
alone on the ocean,
Ellen would need these skills.
If you can repair your boat,
you can stay in the race.

And you can stay alive.

2 *Iduna*

Iduna is the name
of a Viking goddess.
It was also the name
of Ellen's next boat.

Iduna was bigger and faster
than *The Kestrel*.
Ellen took it on her first big solo trip.
She sailed all the way round the UK.

It took her over three months.
This wasn't a race,
and Ellen took her time.

She stopped off in Southampton.
She had to pick up an award.
Ellen had been voted
Young Sailor of the Year.

She was still only 18 years old.

Ellen already knew
what she wanted to do next.

There's a race
called the Mini Transat.
It's a solo race
across the Atlantic
and back again.

Ellen knew she'd need a better boat
to race the Mini Transat.

In a boatyard in France,
Ellen found what she was looking for.
It was called *Le Poisson*
(French for *The Fish*).

It was love at first sight.
As soon as she saw it,
Ellen knew she'd sail *The Fish*
across the world and back.

Ellen climbing the mast.

3 *The Fish*

The Fish was the same size as *Iduna*,
but its mast was much bigger.
A bigger mast means bigger sails.
Bigger sails means you go much faster.

It was going to cost a lot of money.

Ellen lived in a Portakabin
in the boatyard
to save money.
She worked on the boat herself
to save money.

She wrote begging letters,
asking for money.
Ellen sent thousands of letters,
to everyone she could think of.

Her mum and dad gave her a loan.
Her nan left Ellen some money in her will.

Ellen set sail on the Mini Transat
in October 1997.
It was not long after her 21st birthday.

One minute she was on the dockside.
She was talking to people,
saying her goodbyes,
doing last-minute checks.
Next minute she was alone on the sea.

The Fish was only 21 feet (6.5m) long
and 9 feet (3m) wide.

For the next 6,500km (4,000 miles),
Ellen was on her own.

There was no time to relax.
She was fixing ropes, changing sails,
always moving to find the fastest winds.

She slept a little at a time,
steering while she slept.
If she was lucky,
she'd sleep for 20 minutes
before something woke her.

After 24 days at sea,
she finished the race in 13th place.
That was no good.
Ellen had wanted to win!
But it was not bad
for her first solo trip across the world.

Not bad for a 21-year-old girl!
That's what the press said.
They asked Ellen – what was it like
to be the only young girl in the race?

Ellen said: 'I can't say!
I don't think of myself as young.
I don't see myself as a token girl.
I'm a sailor, like the others.

'I have my strong points,
and my weak points.
Just like every other sailor.

'I just want to be treated the same.
When there's a storm at sea,
we all get treated the same!'

Ellen's boat heading for stormy weather.

4 Storm and Calm

When there's a storm at sea . . .

The sky is black with cloud.
The wind rages at 100km an hour.
The rain in your face
stabs like freezing needles.

The waves are 60-metre walls
all round the boat.
The boat rides up the wall of water.
Over the top of it.
Down the other side.

Or the boat crashes into the wave,
and the wave crashes down onto the boat.

There's freezing water everywhere:
in your clothes, in your boots,
in the cabin, in your food,
in your bed.

Sails get ripped to pieces
in the winds.
Boats are buckled and broken
in the waves.
Rudders are smashed.
Masts get snapped off like twigs.

Boats get rolled over on one side.
They get tipped upside down.
You can break an arm, or a rib,
if you get thrown across the cabin.
Men have been swept over the side,
and lost for ever.

'Sometimes,' Ellen says,
'you get a problem up the mast.
A sail gets jammed,
the radio stops working . . .
You have to climb up and sort it out.

'The boat steers itself
and you start to climb.
You keep bashing onto the mast
as the boat rolls into the waves.'

But when the sea is calm . . .

Ellen says:
'You fly over the water.
But it's so calm and still
you don't feel you're moving!

'The air in your lungs
is so fresh and clean.

'The sun on the sea
is like silver and gold.
At night there's the biggest moon
and the brightest stars you ever saw!

'Sailing is hard work.
There's always work to do.
You never get all the sleep you need.

'But you feel free.
There's no-one else for miles.
Just you and the dolphins
and the flying fish . . .

'It's the best feeling in the world!'

5 *Kingfisher*

By the year 2000,
Ellen was in her next new boat:
Kingfisher.

Kingfisher was built for Ellen.
It was brand new.
Everything on board
was the best that money could buy.
It was Ellen's 'work of art'.

Ellen didn't have to worry
about old ropes, or leaks,
or masts that might break.
No more mending second-hand sails!
Kingfisher was a dream come true.

It was built in New Zealand.
Ellen sailed 19,000km back to England.
She got to know *Kingfisher* on the way.

Kingfisher was 60 feet (18m) long.
The biggest boat Ellen had ever had.
But *Kingfisher* was fast.
It sailed without a sound.

It was built for speed.
There were no extras.

There was no kitchen,
just a little sink and a little cooker.
There was no toilet.
No shower. No hot water.
When Ellen slept,
she slept in a chair.

But Ellen loved it.
She said sailing *Kingfisher*
was like meeting an old friend again.
It felt right.
They belonged together.

They got back to England
just in time for her next big race
across the Atlantic:
The Europe 1 New Man Star.

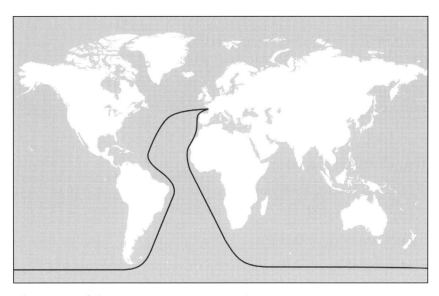

The route of the Europe 1 New Man Star.

For the first eight days of the race,
Ellen was in the lead.
She saw no-one.
Then one morning:
a red sail – just behind her.
Another boat was catching up.

At the end of that day,
Ellen was 120km ahead.
She sailed hard all night.
In the morning,
she was just 8km ahead.

Ellen sailed into fog and icebergs.
She fell, nearly knocked herself out.
One of her sails fell in the sea,
ropes wrapped round *Kingfisher*'s keel.
Ellen lost three hours
getting it free.
She had to stay ahead of the red sail.

After 14 days and 23 hours,
Ellen crossed the finish line
in first place.
She'd won in record time!

6 Ellen's Next Big Race

Ellen's next big race was in 2000/1.
It was called the Vendée Globe
(you say it: Von-day).
The Vendée is the biggest and the best
solo race round the world.

It's also the most dangerous.

Ellen was second all the way.
On 10 January
she was 800km behind.
By 18 January
the gap was just 41km,
with 1,500km still to go . . .
For a time,
Ellen took the lead.
Then she fell behind again.

Ellen came second.
She heard the winner
cross the finish line
on *Kingfisher*'s radio.
Ellen was still 400km out at sea.

She got home a day later.

She'd been at sea for 94 days,
four hours, 25 minutes and 40 seconds.
After more than 38,000km,
alone at sea,
Ellen didn't want it to end.
She didn't want to leave *Kingfisher*.

But the crowds were waiting to see her.
Her mum and dad were waiting to see her.
The film crews were waiting to film her.
The Prime Minister was on the phone.
(Later, Ellen got an MBE.)

Ellen was the fastest woman
to finish the Vendée.
And at 24 years of age,
she was the youngest person
ever to finish the race.

The next year, 2002,
Ellen sailed *Kingfisher* for the last time.
It was another race across the Atlantic.
Ellen won again – in record time.

By now, Ellen was looking
for an even better boat.

Ellen's boat, *Kingfisher*.

7 B&Q

A boat can tip over in a bad storm.
So boats have dagger boards
that stick out the bottom of the hull.
The dagger boards help keep boats upright
and steady in the water.

(In the Vendée, in 2001,
Ellen's dagger board broke.
It cost her the race.)

But if your boat has *two* hulls,
it will be more steady in the water.
You won't need a dagger board.
And if your boat has *three* hulls,
it's even more steady.

Ellen's next boat had three hulls.
B&Q was planned and built
for a short woman like Ellen.
It cost over £1 million.

On 28 November 2004,
Ellen set sail on *B&Q*.
She was sailing solo,
non-stop, round the world.
She wanted to finish
in record time.

Ellen kept a log on the trip.
And she had lots of webcams.
You could follow Ellen
on her website.

 At one point, Ellen wrote:
'The last three days' sailing
have been the worst of my life.
It feels like the sea
is trying to break the boat up.

'The boat is shaking,
and creaking and groaning
and smashing and grinding.
I'm sure something is going to break.'

By 7 February 2005,
she was back in British waters.
After 71 days at sea,
Ellen beat the record
by 1 day and 8 hours.

Thousands of people
came to welcome her back.

The Queen and Prince Charles
both sent messages.
Ellen was made a Dame.
Still only 28,
she was the youngest person
ever to get the award.

'It was hard the whole time,'
Ellen said.
'I have never been
as tired as this in my life.
When I crossed the line,
I just wanted to fall down and sleep!'

A hero: Ellen completes her solo voyage around the world in record time.

8 What Next for Ellen?

Ellen has said:
'If you want to make something happen,
go for it. You can do it.
I just chose to do it in a boat!'

'In 2001,
when I raced in the Vendée Globe
I came second.
It would be good
to enter again and win!
In 2008, maybe –
I'll only be 30 years old…

'There are plenty of records
to be broken.
Across the English Channel.
Across the Atlantic.
Around the world.

'I'm just dying to get back on the water!'